Taming Your Tormenta

A Story About Courage and Hope in the Face of Hurricane María

Jacque Marling de Cuéllar,
M.Ed, LMHC

ORANGE, TX, USA

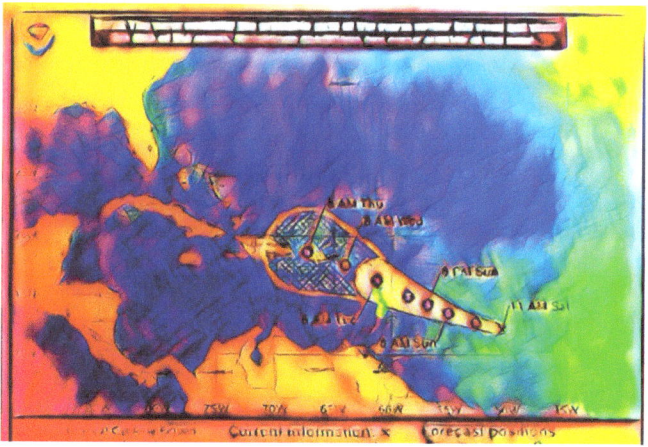

Pictures and Illustration by Jacque Marling de Cuéllar
Editing: Donna Gunter of BizSmartPublishing.com and Cindy Bozek
Spanish Translation: Tania Pesquera Acosta and Maria Otheguy
Illustration Assistant: Adriiana Almestica
Special thank you for the photos contributed by Angel and Delora Saint Kitts, Luis Fonseca, Cynthia Fleishauer, Luz Caban and Zulma Santana Vázquez.

Copyright © 2018 by Jacque Marling de Cuéllar

All rights reserved. No part of this publication may be reproduced, distributed, or transmitted in any form or by any means, without prior written permission.

BizSmart Publishing
Orange, TX, USA 77630
https://www.BizSmartPublishing.com

All rights reserved. No part of this publication may be reproduced, distributed or transmitted in any form or by any means, including photocopying, recording, or other electronic or mechanical methods, without the prior written permission of the publisher, except in the case of brief quotations embodied in critical reviews and certain other noncommercial uses permitted by copyright law. For permission requests, write to the publisher at the website above.

Cover Design © 2018 Nathan Dasco, http://nathanieldasco.com/

Taming Your Tormenta: A Story About Courage and Hope in the Face of Hurricane María / Jacque Marling de Cuéllar. -- 1st ed.
ISBN-13: 978-1-7326998-0-9
ISBN-10: 1-7326998-0-1

Dedication

This book is dedicated in memory of my daughter, Ericka Wilcox. We shared a common passion for rescue dogs, the poet Rumi, and the value of friends and family.

A percentage of the royalties from the retail sales of *Taming Your Tormenta* are donated to El Faro de los Animales, a rescue dog shelter in Humacao, Puerto Rico, in Ericka's memory.

El Faro de los Animales (Lighthouse of the Animals) is a 501c3 non-profit organization that operates a limited capacity adoption center in Humacao, Puerto Rico.

They are dedicated to rehabilitating and sheltering homeless dogs and cats and preparing them for a new home.

Their mission includes bringing to the Puerto Rican population, especially the children, the importance of compassionate treatment towards animals and educating on the need to sterilize and vaccinate their pets.

You can learn more about El Faro by visiting https://elfaropr.org/

Rave Reviews

"I was a college student twenty years ago, experiencing migraine headaches for days due to anxiety and stress. I was referred to Jacque and felt a connection immediately. She was compassionate and saw me for who I was.

Jacque made a huge impact on my life. I was in a place of hopelessness and self-hate. My father had passed away over a year before I went to MCLA, and I was filled with grief. Jacque connected me to a bereavement group, which was so helpful. She helped me feel like a real person who deserved to feel healthy.

Overall, my life is better because she believed in me from the beginning, which helped me believe in myself. She taught me the importance of self-care and mindfulness. Twenty years later, I still use coping skills Jacque taught me. If it weren't for Jacque, I would not have graduated from MCLA. I would recommend Jacque to anyone." ~~*Susie, Massachusetts College of Liberal Arts alumni*

"I can't say enough good about this program. My daughter, Rayne, shared her story with Jacque as we participated in Jacque's mindfulness program. The program focuses on how to deal with any type of stress or anxiety. Rayne was pretty good through the hurricane, but she didn't have the tools to process the anxiety afterward. This program has given her confidence and specific skills and exercises to help her process the fears and concerns that come up as we continue our lives. These skills will be with our kids their whole lives, making them stronger and more centered as they go through school, work, and interpersonal situations." ~~*Sabrina Parks, mother of Rayne*

Preface

Dear Readers:

This book is a tribute to the children of Puerto Rico and a message of resilience in the face of trauma, whether it be storms, fire, shootings, or natural or personal disasters. Focusing on a positive memory while doing something like holding a glitter bottle, doing a walking meditation, tapping, or just belly-breathing are all strategies you can use to help calm yourself when things begin to feel overwhelming.

If you are calm and feeling safe, then you can make better decisions and keep yourself and others safe. You cannot panic if you are belly-breathing, doing walking meditation, or tapping and being present in the moment. These strategies can be used for everyone, victims, and trauma workers alike. If you can take care of yourself and be calm in the moment, you will be resilient and safe.

Research has proven that meditation, prayer, and self-care reduce the incidence of post-traumatic stress disorder (PTSD). Best-selling author Nick Ortner defines resiliency as "the capacity to recover quickly from difficulties; toughness." Resiliency is a critical life skill that makes all the difference between feeling like you have been run over by life and feeling like you have some control of your life.

The good news is that resiliency is a muscle that you can actively strengthen and improve with practice. The story in this book will help you build your resiliency muscles.

Here's to taming your tormenta! Breathe Deep! Stay Present!

Jacque Marling de Cuéllar

Contents

The Tormenta Arrives 11
Aurianna's Story: Be Prepared 23
Building Self-Care Life Skills 29
Pelusa's Story: Ask for Help 37
Rayne's Story: Life's Problems-A Puzzle to Solve............................. 41
How to Experience and Use Taming Your Tormenta with Children....49
Mindfulness Activity: Belly Breathing 54
Mindfulness Activity: Make a Glitter Bottle 55
Afterword: What Inspired Me to Write This Book 56

Hand outstretched in the sunshine
Hoping you would pause, albeit briefly
A moment of gratitude and joy
As your long hello reminded me to trust
Trust in myself and the power of the light
For the lights will always
hold me when I falter.

ericka r. wilcox

CHAPTER ONE

―

The Tormenta Arrives

ONCE UPON A TIME on the beautiful island of Puerto Rico, U.S.A., on September 20, 2017...

...a Tormenta named María was approaching the island, a hurricane of mass destruction.

Some families fled the island to seek safety.

But many could not leave. So, families prepared as best they could to keep their children and families safe.

During the hurricane, children and families had many feelings. For hours upon hours, this Tormenta blew her fiery, wet breath.

María's breath was so powerful and scary. She wreaked havoc with destruction and uncertainty.

Day after day, no one knew what was going to happen. The sky was gray for three days, and time stopped. People felt numb.

There was no food, no water, no electricity, and no gas. People stood in the blistering, hot sun for supplies.

Sometimes viewing bad things from a distance in our mind helps heal memories.

People managed downed power lines and waded through flood waters to stay safe.

María destroyed everything in her path - beaches, houses, churches, playgrounds, and cars. Even the rain forest was stripped of its leaves and trees.

Recovery Takes Time.

Eleven months later after the storm had passed, many families were still coping with no electricity and blue tarp roofs. Recovery happens one day at a time.

Monkey Island, or El Cayo de Punta Santiago, is now two islands instead of one because of the terrible wind and rain. Yet, the monkeys survived.

And nature thrived to grow anew, as did the children of Puerto Rico.

CHAPTER TWO

―

Aurianna's Story: Be Prepared

AURIANNA IS 9 YEARS old and lives in Punta Santiago, Puerto Rico. She and her family still had no electricity eight months after the hurricane.

During the hurricane, Aurianna felt safe because her *mami* and her *papi* were prepared and stayed calm.

Teacher Jacque was visiting Aurianna's parents. They were talking about Jacque's program, *Taming Your Dragon's Breath, Taming Your Tormenta*.

Aurianna heard the instructions of how to make a glitter bottle to use to calm her Dragon's Breath.

On her own, she made a glitter bottle for herself and the little girl next door, who was five years old.

Even though daily life was a struggle, Aurianna would wake up and sing. "Mi amor, Puerto Rico." ("I love you, Puerto Rico.")

Like the island's coquis, Aurianna's childlike voice sang a song, a message of love, hope, action and caring for others.

Though Hurricane María destroyed many things, the spirit and faith of the children and families did survive.

Planting the Seeds for New Growth.

CHAPTER THREE

Building Self-Care Life Skills

AFTER THE HURRICANE, TEACHER Jacque introduced a meditation program, *Taming your Dragon's Breath, Taming your Tormenta* in school.

Children learned to pay attention to their breath and develop a sense of calm.

Sometimes children have to be reminded to let go of the Dragon feelings Hurricane María left behind.

Remember a feeling of still being safe after something bad happens. Children can learn to pay attention to their breath and focus their thoughts.

You can relax the muscles in your body and quiet your thoughts. Listen to your body when it tells you if you are hungry, need to sleep, need a hug, or need to ask for help.

Breathe deep into your belly and quiet your mind. You can notice and allow your thoughts to wander.

Allow your thoughts to drift on white fluffy clouds, especially the scary ones. Comfort yourself, say, "They are just thoughts and I am safe."

But the children said, "¡Pero, pero...!"

"What if I am not safe?"

Remember, breathe in through your nose, deep into your belly. Hold for a moment and then slowly blow out through your mouth your Dragon's Breath. Allow yourself feelings of comfort and safety.

Ask yourself, "What do I need? Do I need a hug? Do I need to talk to my parents, my teachers or my friends? Do I need to pray? Do I need to play? Do I need to eat or sleep? Am I safe?"

If you name and honor your feelings and quiet your mind, you will know what to do in an emergency. You now know to ask for help and tame your Dragon's Breath.

CHAPTER FOUR

Pelusa's Story: Ask for Help

A LITTLE WARM, SOFT, friendly service dog named Pelusa visited the children in school. Pelusa shows you how to recognize when you are safe and when you are not.

When Pelusa heard the popping of the bursting balloons, she felt it sounded like gunfire. She became frightened and did not know she was safe. She began to shake and tremble.

Yet, she was safe, and she too had survived.

She was a smart little dog, and she learned how to ask for help. Pelusa allowed Adriiana to comfort her until her body and Dragon's Breath calmed down.

You, too, can learn to calm your Dragon's Breath and accept help. Breathe into your belly. Allow yourself to accept help and recognize you are safe. Remember Pelusa's lesson.

CHAPTER FIVE

Rayne's Story: Life's Problems-A Puzzle to Solve

RAYNE IS 7 YEARS old and lives in Humacao, Puerto Rico. She colored and played with her toys during the hurricane.

Rayne's house started to shake. Rayne said, "Mami, the house is shaking." Her madre said, "I don't feel the house shaking." That is when Rayne became really scared, because she knew the house was shaking.

When grownups are truthful and allow children to have all kinds of feelings, even sad ones and bad ones, children will be okay.

She said, "But Mami, the house is really shaking."

Raynes's *madre* said, "You are right, Rayne. The house is really shaking. You should trust your instincts, but it is a very strong house and we are safe."

Rayne felt safe again and knew she was okay.

Rayne's *mami* was a good *mami*. She wanted to protect her daughter.

Like all good mamis, she knew sometimes parents can't always protect their children. She realized her job was to teach Rayne to be resilient and tame her Dragon's Breath so Rayne would be prepared for life's events.

Rayne was taught to think of problems like a puzzle to solve and to ask for help. She had faith she would find a solution. You can, too.

Rayne tuned out and turned down in her mind the scary sound of the wind and rain. Rayne learned she could not control the hurricane.

She could control how she reacted by calming her Dragon's Breath. She asked for help, cuddled with her *mami*, played, and stayed in the present moment.

Now, it is time to end this chapter of *Taming your Tormenta's Breath*. There will be many more stories from the children to unfold like an orchid in the spring, showing its beauty and strength.

Until next time, put your hand over your heart and a hand on your belly. Breathe in and breathe out. Notice all your feeling of good and bad in life, because in this moment, you are safe.

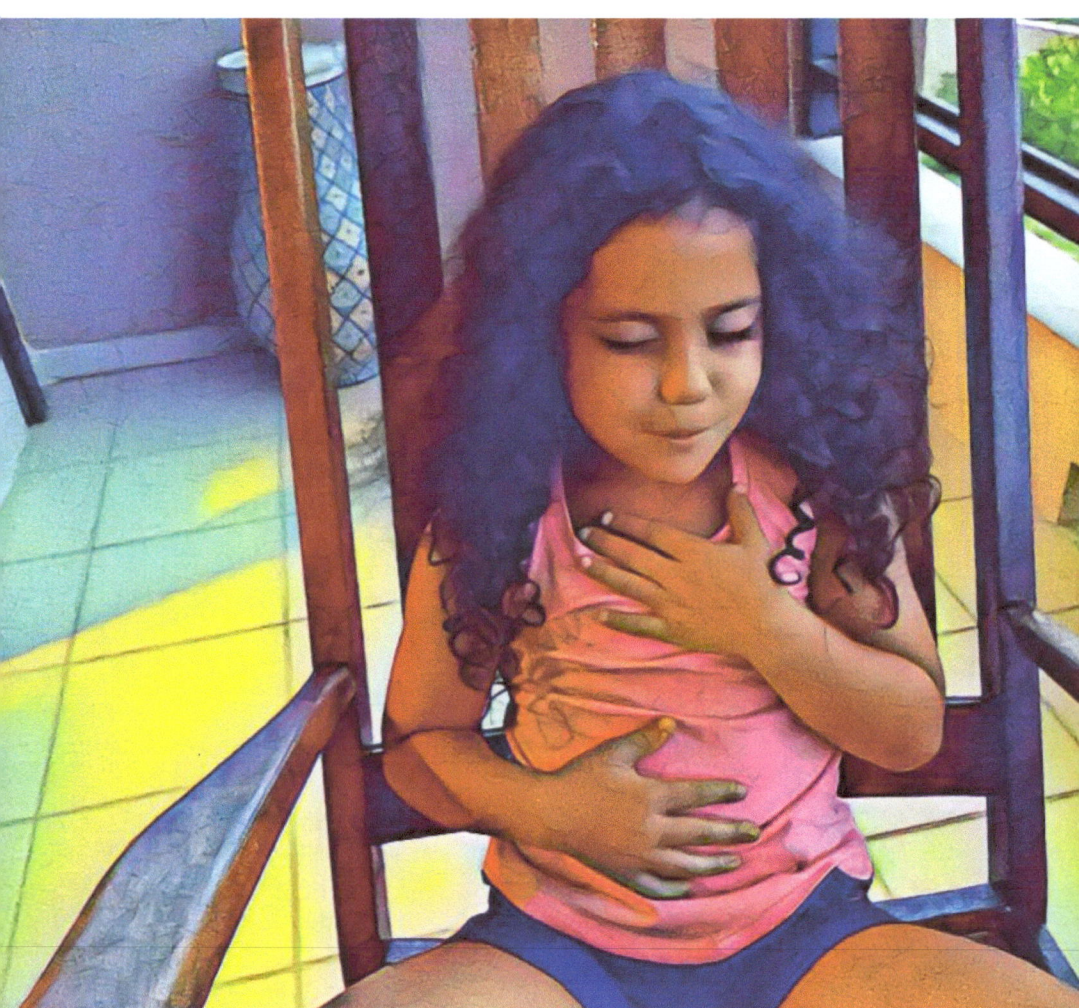

How to Experience and Use Taming Your Tormenta with Children

I suggest that you read *Taming Your Tormenta* first before you read the book with children. Know if you have experienced a loss, this book may bring up feelings that may need attention. This book is meant to be an experience with children, so if they have any questions or need support, you will be available to help. It is okay to share your feelings and coping strategies for grief and loss to give children a real-life example and model how to manage emotions. If you are a volunteer, teacher, or therapist teaching belly breathing or mindfulness activities, you can also use these guidelines when reading this story.

Although the hurricane has passed, windy days and howling winds trigger some people's memories of Hurricane María and its aftermath. Become aware of what triggers your extreme emotions like guilt, shame, fear, contempt, disgust, anger, sadness, surprise, anxiety, confusion, envy, horror, nostalgia, or embarrassment. Awareness helps you understand your mood so you can develop a plan for calming and coping. Having a routine of healthy self-care habits allows your body, mind, and spirit to heal. It is common to feel afraid during and after a traumatic event. This fight-flight-freeze response is a normal reaction meant to protect a person from harm. Your emotions are not a character flaw but a natural instinctive state of mind in response to a traumatic event.

Bessel Van Kolk, M.D., states, "Trauma is neither a disease nor a disorder, but rather an injury caused by fright, helplessness, and loss. Trauma that results in injuries can be transformed and healed by attending to the natural healing powers that reside deep within every human being."

A year and a half after Hurricane María, my friend, Greg, was still very bothered by the howling wind. One day while visiting his brother, the wind began to howl, and things began to rattle. Greg put his hands over his face and said, "I just can't take the sound of the howling wind." His brother reminded him that in the present moment, he was safe. His brother suggested to think of the wind differently and to tell himself, "I love the wind, I love the wind." Now,

Greg says to himself, "I love the wind. I love the sound of the wind." He also reminds himself he survived the last hurricane, and he will know what to do in the future to continue to keep his family safe and mentally healthy. On a recent windy day, he realized he was not reacting or feeling anxious, and that he felt safe.

Self-care, belly breathing, meditation, and mindfulness activities help calm and reset that flight-flight-freeze response. I tell you this story to remind you it is essential to pay attention to self-talk, or what we say to ourselves for our robust mental health. Greg's story is an example of how you can share your feelings with someone you trust, become aware of what triggers your extreme emotions, and have a willingness to change your thoughts.

An elderly lady told me that reading *Domando Tu Tormenta* helped her grieve some of her losses. She dealt solely with practical issues the first year after Hurricane María, things like putting her life and household back together, and only doing what had to be done. A year and a half after the storm, she was surprised to acknowledge how consumed she was with a deep sense of sadness. Realizing she had to move forward in the grieving process, she would read a small portion of the book, put it down, cry, and then go back to it later. This is an example of how she permitted herself to experience her feelings of loss slowly over time.

Grieving is a process that can take time - weeks, months, years. The intensity of your emotions will diminish and pass over time; they are just part of a normal cycle of recovery. Everyone grieves differently when they have experienced a significant loss in their life. You may experience some, all, or none of the emotions of denial, anger, sadness, depression, helplessness, guilt, or a sense of relief. You may experience other feelings, as well. Recognize what might be considered a small disaster for adults, like the loss of a favorite toy, may be experienced as a significant loss by a child.

One five-year-old boy, Michael, felt sad because his goldfish died after the hurricane. His family helped him bury his fish in a box in their back yard. The burial, ensuing conversation, and acknowledgment of his loss were opportunities to discuss how death is part of the human life cycle, and this ceremony served to support his experience. A support system, self-care, traditions, or rituals allow you to heal over time.

I was supposed to be on the island during Hurricane María, but instead, I was in Massachusetts caring for my terminally ill daughter, Ericka. She was suddenly diagnosed in September 2017 with ovarian cancer and died six weeks later, October 15, 2017. As I knew I could not save or protect my daughter, I decided to focus my energy on loving her and helping others. Taking action allowed me to shake off the traumatic power of feeling hopeless about all the loss occurring around me. In February 2018, I began presenting meditation stress-reducing workshops, helping the children of Puerto Rico. *Taming Your Tormenta* was the result of attending to my grief as well as emotions of anger and sadness. The book is dedicated to Ericka, and one of her poems is at the beginning of the book.

Although this story centers on Hurricane María that devastated Puerto Rico on September 20, 2017, the lessons are relevant to anyone who has ever experienced a hurricane or any natural disaster.

Chapter 1: The Tormenta Arrives

If you are a parent, you can read with your child and use the first chapter to have a conversation about how your child feels about Hurricane María now that some time has passed. Sometimes just listening and allowing them to express how they feel is enough. Sometimes your children might not want to talk about it, or they might not be ready. That is okay, too; let them feel comfortable sharing or not. Or, your children may still have fears; they might need reassurance and a reminder that in this present moment, they are safe, and their feelings are normal. Sometimes prayer or reliance on family values or spiritual practices is enough; it depends on the child and the family.

This chapter acknowledges the historical event of Puerto Rican people surviving Hurricane María. I want to convey a message of hope and survival in spite of the devastation, as well as a reminder recovery happens over time and occurs one day at a time. I have included several images from nature to encourage children to visualize as a symbol of recovery and growth.

Chapter 2: Aurianna's Story: Be Prepared

This chapter illustrates when bad things happen, children will be okay if parents can remain calm. The family in this chapter prepared as best they could. After the hurricane, their focus was to survive, keep a routine, maintain their faith, and help others. The lesson is our children are always listening to what we are saying and observing what we do. Even though children may be young, they can be of service and help others. Allowing and encouraging your child to help others is a compelling role to build their self-esteem.

Chapter 3: Building Self-Care Life Skills

Chapter three is about self-care, (eating healthy, sleeping, exercising) and practicing mindfulness exercises to calm and soothe yourself. Using a glitter bottle and belly breathing are examples of mindfulness exercises, as are using your thoughts to calm yourself, as well as using questions to recognize when you are safe and when you are not.

You may notice multiple photos of a blue tarp being used in my workshops throughout this chapter. For those never having experienced a hurricane, a blue tarp is what FEMA (Federal Emergency Management Agency) issues to homeowners to protect their home if it was damaged during the hurricane and needs repair. The use of the blue tarp in all of my workshops is a symbol to honor the strength and resilience of Puerto Rico and to encourage children to be proud even if they have a blue -tarp roof.

Chapter 4: Pelusa's Story: Ask for Help

Chapter four uses the story of Pelusa, my dog, to learn to ask for and accept help, as well as a reminder to recognize when you are safe. The story in the chapter about the popping balloons and Pelusa becoming afraid and then jumping into a student's lap actually occurred in the classroom in Cidra.

It was a teachable moment. I stopped the workshop to tell the students Pelusa was giving them an example of what to do when you are afraid, and that is: asking for help.

Chapter 5: Rayne's Story: Life's Problems – A Puzzle to Solve

This chapter demonstrates parents are not perfect, and the best we can do is learn from our mistakes and be truthful about life events. It acknowledges a parent cannot always protect their children from harm and life events. This fact is a part of life; we are human. Be kind to yourself. One of our jobs as parents is to nurture and teach our children and use the definition of resilience (capacity to recover quickly from difficulties; toughness) to help our children grow and develop.

Here's how to use the notion of resilience with your children:

- Look at problems like a puzzle to solve.
- Identify what you can control and what you cannot control.
- Ask for help from people that will be on your team and support you.
- Make a plan and be willing to change the plan if needed.

The guidelines outlined in this book are not a substitution for therapy. The messages in this book are life skills that can benefit both children and adults. While there are many mindfulness exercises in this book, I have introduced only two, belly breathing and how to make a glitter bottle. I chose these because these mindfulness exercises are simple to make and easy to do. Children always have their breath and imagination with them.

Download the book bonus at
https://www.jacquemarling.com/bookbonus.html

Mindfulness Activity: Belly Breathing

Parents, children, and adolescents can learn and practice mindfulness as part of daily life to improve and support mental health, self-care, and well-being. The goal is to teach simple, practical skills to help individuals cope with life pressures they face in their lives.

People benefit from mindfulness exercises, breathing exercises, relaxing techniques, guided imagery, and other methods to help to regulate their emotions.

One long-term goal is for children to be introduced consistently to mindfulness at a young age and use the skills throughout their school years into adulthood. These methods provide children and adolescents the opportunity to develop life skills to thrive, be resilient, and master the challenges of today's modern world.

Children and adult's good health improves behaviorally over time, using daily life mindfulness activities through the use of play, imagery, gratitude, journaling, connecting with nature, community service, and team building. Repetition of mindfulness activities sets the foundation to develop healthy habits and coping techniques for life. This belly breathing exercise is one activity you can do together and experience with your child.

How to Do Belly Breathing

Belly breathing is easy to do and can be relaxing. Try this basic exercise and make it a daily habit. Use this exercise any time you need to relax, take a break, or relieve stress.

1. Sit or lie in a comfortable position.
2. Put one hand on your belly over your belly button and the other hand over your heart or chest.
3. Take a deep breath in through your nose and let your breath fill your belly like a balloon.
4. Breathe out through your pursed lips (like fish lips) as if you were blowing out candles or blowing bubbles.
5. Do this breathing 3 to 10 times. Take your time with each breath.
6. Notice how you feel at the end of the exercise.

Mindfulness Activity: Make a Glitter Bottle

Try this basic activity and use a glitter bottle any time you need to relax, take a break, or relieve stress.

Having busy thoughts in our mind is normal. Children and adults benefit from mindfulness exercises, breathing exercises, relaxation techniques, guided imagery, and other methods to help regulate their mood. A glitter bottle can be used to calm your thoughts and feelings. The swirling glitter is like a windy storm in our mind when things become busy. It happens when we are distracted, worried, angry, or stressed out. Your thoughts and feelings are like the swirling glitter when you feel overwhelmed or think too much.

A glitter bottle is simple to make. You can use a plastic water bottle. Remove the wrapping. Pour a little glitter into the bottle of water. Put superglue inside of the cap. Seal tightly.

Shake your bottle to see the glitter fly around. Watch the glitter swirl and slowly float to the bottom of the bottle. Keep watching the glitter. Breathe slowly as you watch. When you practice mindfulness belly breathing and focus on positive thoughts while watching the glitter, it allows your mind to relax and calm down.

Download the book bonus at
https://www.jacquemarling.com/bookbonus.html

Afterword: What Inspired Me to Write This Book

I've always viewed Puerto Rico as my beautiful island retreat where I go to rest and restore my soul. The devastating impact of the storm was so evident. I knew so many people who had lost everything. It was heartbreaking to experience the transformation of the island from a tranquil paradise to something that resembled a war zone.

When you personally know people who have lost everything, you can't help but be compelled to want to do something. I successfully initiated a clothing drive within the community in which I live, Palmas del Mar, Puerto Rico. The residents there were very generous with clothing and money, and in a small way, we were able to help a number of people begin to put their homes and lives back together.

However, the clothing drive still didn't feel like enough. I continued to ask myself what else could I do or offer that would help make a difference in the lives of the families of Puerto Rico. I have expertise in trauma recovery and the ability to reach and help as many people as possible in a very simple way using play and self-care life skills.

In work with survivors of Hurricane Katrina in 2005, counselors and trauma workers discovered if parents are okay, remain calm, and take action, their children will mirror that behavior. Research indicates that meditation, mindfulness, prayer, and self-care are instrumental in people managing and recovering from trauma.

For thirty years in my career as a therapist, I have been writing stories and therapeutic metaphors for my clients and empowering others to create a life they love. I taught these life self-care skills to my own children, so it seemed natural for me to offer my expertise to the hurricane survivors.

I asked my neighbor and friend, Rebecca, what more I could do. She introduced me to her daughter, Melba Passapera, who runs a program called "Open Doors" (Puertas Abiertas) at the school, Luis Munoz Iglesias in Cidra, Puerto Rico. I began visiting the Cidra school and introduced my "Taming Your Dragon" program.

I was deeply moved by the children sharing their stories and their responses to my one-word lesson plan to describe their experience. After my very first workshop, I began to write the story in this book.

I returned to the classroom several times to teach wellness lessons and read this story to the kids. In Cidra and Punta Santiago, the kids had never experienced this type of workshop; it seemed to make a difference. The kids eagerly participated, and parents joined in as well.

I also attended a fundraising luncheon in which the proceeds were being donated to the hurricane relief efforts. My newfound friend, Sabrina, approached me after the luncheon and asked about offering a workshop in Palmas del Mar. My workshops in Cidra and the workshop Sabrina hosted were the geneses of the programs I am now offering to the schools and community.

The generosity of the community has been instrumental for me to offer these life skills and make this book possible. My neighbor, Nydia, sent her granddaughters to me and we made 50 glitter bottles. They blew up 60 balloons and participated in the workshops, as well. Lillian transported kids, balloons, and supplies. Tania translated the book and Luz read the story in Spanish. Cindy and Adriiana helped with tech support. Rebecca transported me, fed me, and gave me wise advice. Sabrina was my sounding board. My long-term friends, Angel, Delora, Welchito, and Cynthia have been a valuable support. I also want to thank longtime friend and trusted confidant, Donna Gunter, who is a wonderful, terrific, skilled expert, and without whose help this book would not have been possible. I thank you all, to name a few. I am thankful to be a part of this wonderful community.

And last but not least, I need to thank my wonderful husband, David Milewski. This book would not be possible without his unparalleled devotion and love for me, as well as for his eternal patience with me and ongoing caretaking he does on my behalf. My life would not be what it is today without him. Everyone who has volunteered in this work walks away blessed.

You experience first-hand the destruction, pain, and struggle, and you stand in awe as families, friends, and communities help each other and rebuild their lives. The resilience and generosity of others who have had, at different times, very little, is immeasurable. This speaks to the spirit and essence of the people of Puerto Rico.

I want to encourage those of you who are teachers, therapists, yoga instructors, or just someone who practices meditation to take your vacation in Puerto Rico. Take some time to adopt a school and go play with the kids and teach them meditation.

Trust me, you will reap more rewards than you sow.

With deep gratitude,

Jacque Marling de Cuéllar

ABOUT THE AUTHOR

    Jacque Marling de Cuéllar is a licensed therapist, board certified clinical Ericksonian hypnotherapist, and life coach with more than 30 years' experience. Previously she practiced at Massachusetts College of Liberal Arts and continues to maintain her own private practice. Her mission and purpose are to help others who suffer from trauma, anxiety, depression, cancer, and brain injury. She works with her clients to create a sense of hope that life can be different and specializes in working with individuals teaching wellness and self-care to create a life they love.

    Jacque is a breast cancer survivor. For those who suffer from cancer and chronic illness, Jacque utilizes a multi-disciplinary approach such as hypnosis, meditation, progressive relaxation to help you to create a quality of life. She offers one-on-one coaching, workshops, and customized programs for clients seeking to create the life they desire.

    Jacque has a master's degree from the University of Massachusetts - Amherst and is a licensed mental health counselor. She is a board-certified clinical hypnotherapist from the American Hypnosis Academy in Silver Spring, MD, and neuro-linguistic practitioner.

She divides her time between her homes in Massachusetts and Puerto Rico.

Contact the Author:
Website: https://www.JacqueMarling.com
Facebook: https://www.facebook.com/BusyBodiesQuietMinds/
Twitter: https://twitter.com/jacquemarling
LinkedIn: https://www.linkedin.com/in/jacquemarling/
Pinterest: https://id.pinterest.com/jacque_marling/

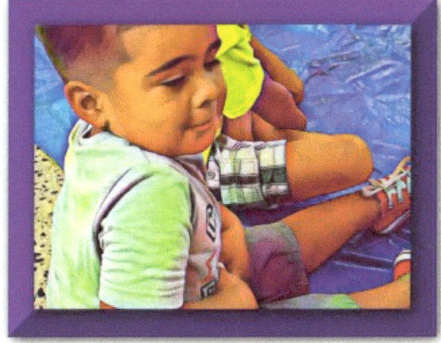

1